MW01492710

Truman - A Special Dog

By Minnie C.Gallman

Photographs by Minnie C. Gallman,
Guiding Eyes For The Blind, and Barry
Newmiller

Cover Photograph by Kevin Kurdzlolek

Copyright © 2013 Minnie C. Gallman

ISBN - 978-1482564242

Dedicated to all the raisers, trainers, and staff that make it possible for the blind to receive Guide Dogs. These dogs provide a priceless gift – independence, companionship, and mobility

Truman's Mom and Dad

Angie

Jeb

I was born today.

Five brothers and two sisters
share my birthday.

I can't see my mother, brothers,
and sisters because my eyes will
not open for eight days.

My world is dark. Every time
I move, I bump into a
brother or a sister.

A soft voice says my
name is Truman.

My sisters are named Tiffany
and Treasure. My brothers are
named Taft, Tommy, Tuffy,
Tempo, and Timmy.

I'm the one in the
middle of the picture.

My eyes are open.
I can see my mother,
brothers, and sisters.

We can play with each other.
Then we all take a nap.

I'm now eight weeks old.

It is time for a checkup. A man in
a white coat looks inside my ears,
listens to my heart, and flashes
a light in my eyes.

He says "What a healthy puppy!
You're going to be a
SPECIAL DOG."
I don't know what that means!

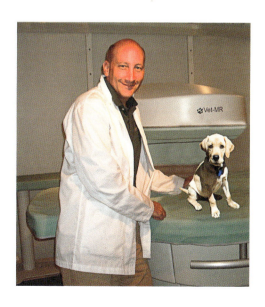

A family comes to the kennel
and takes me to their home.

I have a big back yard,
my own food dish, and
lots of toys.

They even give me a bath.

I thought it would be more fun.

Each day my people spend time
teaching me new words.

When I hear "sit," I am
supposed to sit down.

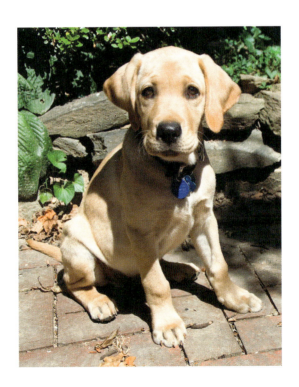

When someone says my name and "come," I'm supposed to go to them and sit at their feet.

I listen most of the time.

My people like to take
me to new places.

Today I went sailing.
It was a lot of fun.

Another day, I met a new friend.

He has big ears like me.

Every week I ride in the car to a
place where there are
other puppies.

We get a chance to play
with each other.

Then we play games with
our people.

I am learning not to
jump on people.

Here I am sitting quietly when a
person comes up to greet me.

Sometimes class is boring.

Now I'm a year old.

I learn more words every day.

I no longer pull on the leash
when we go for walks.

I now know what to do when
my person says "stay" or "heel."

I no longer chase birds and
squirrels when we go on walks.

I'm 16 months old.

My people take me on a long
car ride back to the place
where I was born.

I hear someone say
"Let the test begin."

They pop open an umbrella to
see if it frightens me.
It doesn't.
Then they drop some pots and
pans. I run over to check
them out.

Then I hear the words
"You're a **SPECIAL DOG**."

I still don't know what
that means.

Every day a person called a trainer takes me for a walk.

Instead of a leash, my trainer holds onto a harness.

I don't understand why my trainer runs into things. She seems to have hers eyes closed.

She reminds me of how I couldn't see when I was born.

I realize it is my duty to keep her safe. I need to make sure she doesn't run into things or hit her head on an overhang.

I'm introduced to a new person
who is holding a white cane.

She calls my name and I go over
to her. I sleep next to her bed
and we are always together.

She acts just like my trainer
when she closed her eyes.

It's up to me to make sure she
doesn't trip and can cross the
street safely.

When we go for a walk she
leaves her white cane behind.
I realize she can't see.
I am her eyes.

Now I know what it means
to be a **SPECIAL DOG**.

Truman

More Information:

Truman was born in the Guiding Eyes for the Blind Canine Development Center in Patterson, NY. At eight weeks of age, the pups are tested and those that pass are placed with puppy raisers.

Puppy raisers include a broad spectrum of caring individuals from various walks of life: couples, families with children, young adults, and senior citizens. Raisers provide hours of patient teaching and numerous socialization journeys over a 12 to 16 month period. They return a well-socialized young adult dog to Guiding Eyes' training staff at the Training School in Yorktown Heights, NY. Truman was raised in Northern Virginia. After a pup passes the In-For-Training evaluations, those destined for guide work will begin training with their professional instructors.

The final step is when a blind person receives their priceless gift – a guide dog providing independence, companionship, and mobility.

Guiding Eyes by the Numbers:

Founded: 1954

Graduated guide dogs teams: 7,400

Active Guide Dog graduates: 1,000

Active Heeling Autism graduates: 43

Volunteers: 11,400 people residing in 13 states.

Cost per dog: Approximately $45,000 to breed, raise, train and match a dog. Both guide dogs and autism service dogs are provided to their handlers at no charge.

www.guidingeyes.org
www.facebook.com/guidingeyes@guidingeyes

About the Author:

Minnie Gallman has volunteered as a Puppy sitter with Guiding Eyes For The Blind for 20 years. She has welcomed over a hundred puppies to her home in Northern Virginia. Many of the puppies have sailed with her and her husband on Chesapeake Bay. Minnie's other hobby is photography and the puppies are wonderful subjects.

18005556R00017

Made in the USA
Charleston, SC
11 March 2013